HAL LEONARD KEYBOARD STYLE SERIES

JAZZ-ROCK KEYBOARD

THE COMPLETE GUIDE WITH CD!

BY T LAVITZ

ISBN-13: 978-0-634-03428-2
ISBN-10: 0-634-03428-6

HAL•LEONARD®
CORPORATION

7777 W. BLUEMOUND RD. P.O. BOX 13819 MILWAUKEE, WI 53213

In Australia Contact:
Hal Leonard Australia Pty. Ltd.
4 Lentara Court
Cheltenham, Victoria, 3192 Australia
Email: ausadmin@halleonard.com

Visit Hal Leonard Online at
www.halleonard.com

INTRODUCTION

Welcome to *Jazz-Rock Keyboard*. If you're interested in what makes jazz-rock such a unique and special genre for keyboardists, then you've come to the right place! This book and CD were designed to help keyboardists ranging in levels from intermediate to advanced.

I want to thank Jeff Schroedl, Dan Maske, Charylu Roberts, Alwin Bastiaansen, and everyone at Hal Leonard for making this project available to you. Also, a very special thank you to Wade Starnes for helping with the musical transcriptions and mixing the audio examples, as well as for his overall and never-ending dedication. Thanks, Wade!

Lastly, very important to me is the support I have gotten over the years from my family, friends, and fans. Thanks, everyone!

About the CD

On the accompanying CD, you'll find demonstrations of many of the musical examples in the book. Please see the individual chapters for specific information on the CD tracks and how to use them.

About the Author

T Lavitz was born on April 16, 1956 in Lakewood, New Jersey. After ten years of classical training, T attended the prestigious high school of the arts, the Interlochen Arts Academy, followed by a "Studio Music and Jazz" major at the University of Miami in Coral Gables, Florida. It was there that Lavitz was in good company, which included Jaco Pastorius, Danny Gottlieb, Marc Egan, Bruce Hornsby, and the members of what would become the Dixie Dregs. Almost twenty-nine years and six GRAMMY® nominations later, T is still the keyboardist for the Dregs. Besides the GRAMMYs, this association led to winning "Best New Talent" in 1981 and "Best Jazz Keyboardist" in 1992 by voters in the *Keyboard Magazine* reader's poll. Currently, Magnatude (Magna Carta) Records released T's latest recording as a bandleader. His seventh CD as a producer and composer, the new album *School of the Arts* features Dave Weckl, John Patitucci, Frank Gambale, Steve Morse, and Jerry Goodman.

CONTENTS

Chapter 1
WHAT IS JAZZ-ROCK?

Jazz-Rock is a hybrid of music made up of characteristics of two styles of already existing genres: jazz and rock. Although it may be considered one of the types of *fusion*, it is primarily comprised of only the aforementioned two genres. When people refer to **fusion** or **jazz fusion** (or the redundant moniker **jazz-rock fusion**), they usually mean jazz-rock. However, in actuality the word "fusion" only means to combine two elements, or in the case of music, two (or more) styles. Therefore, one should note that jazz-rock is a fusion, but one particular style of fusion. There are other ways of combining musical genres; for example, country rock or Latin jazz. This book however is focused on the pairing of rock and jazz.

Every decade seems to bring on change and the morphing of multiple musical styles. By the 1950s, jazz was in full bloom, leaving in its wake styles such as Dixieland, and substituting swing beats for the older two-step approach. Drummers started to "ride" on open cymbals, while the bass players embraced walking bass lines. This also allowed for a whole new melodic approach. Saxophonists like Charlie Parker and Lester Young were playing longer lines during their improvisations, moving into what was until then, uncharted territory. One of the musicians who shared the bandstand was Miles Davis. Miles gets a lot of credit when it comes to the formation of jazz-rock. He bridged the gap in a blatant way by tossing in elements of rock into the already progressive jazz mix. Miles made a few landmark contributions to what became the changing of the guard, including his albums *In a Silent Way* and *Bitches Brew* (1969), and then *A Tribute to Jack Johnson* (1970). Once these albums were released, it seemed as though there was no turning back, and a completely different approach to modern music took over.

The lineage is (although perhaps arguably) straightforward after that. Some questions will always remain as to "who did what first," but there is some collaboration that speaks loudly on behalf of the jazz-rock unification. Drummer Tony Williams played with Miles Davis as a teenager, and shortly afterward formed his group Lifetime. Among those who played with him was guitarist John McLaughlin who also gets a lot of credit for the birth of jazz-rock. In 1971 his band the Mahavishnu Orchestra released *Inner Mounting Flame*. This album along with the subsequent *Birds of Fire* (1972) goes down in history to many fans as the pinnacle of jazz-rock. Along with Jan Hammer, Jerry Goodman, Rick Laird, and Billy Cobham, McLaughlin blazed a new trail that is still being followed today. Guitarist Steve Morse said that Mahavishnu's music was the model for his six-time GRAMMY nominated band the Dixie Dregs. To some, the "Dregs" took the Mahavishnu concept even further, adding country jazz and classical styles to the repertoire. The Dixie Dregs are credited by members of the heavy-metal fusion group Dream Theater as their influence when answering their own calling in music. Thus the family tree of jazz-rock continues to flourish.

Guitar, bass, and drums seem to be the instruments in the forefront when it comes to rock music, and often times in jazz as well. In typical rock 'n' roll, this lineup remains fairly consistent, along with (of course) vocals and keyboards. The piano (and electric piano), organ, clavinet, and synthesizers in most vocal rock bands seemed to play more of a supporting rather than leading role. When jazz and rock began to be fused, the keyboardists began to step out, claiming more of the spotlight.

While guitarist John McLaughlin was playing with Mahavishnu, Joe Zawinul forged a new sound for keyboard players with Weather Report, whose self-titled debut was released in 1971. On the average, Weather Report would release one album each year for the next fifteen years, and during the mid 1970s, they dominated the jazz-rock market. In 1977, the band's signature hit song "Birdland" even crossed over to mainstream rock radio stations. It was events like this that helped initiate the ardent rock 'n' roll listener to the fusion of jazz and rock, and to the realization that vocals aren't always necessary to make a piece of music complete.

In 1973 two of the masters of keyboard playing, Herbie Hancock and Chick Corea, entered the ring of electronic crossover music. Hancock had been very popular during the 1960s, both as a band member with Miles Davis and as a solo artist. As a matter of fact, from the beginning of his career as a leader, he was popular on jazz and R&B radio stations. It was the release of *Headhunters* in 1973 that catapulted him to mainstream stardom. This album became the first-ever jazz recording to go platinum. The follow-up recording *Thrust* was much more than just another great instrumental album, but also a comprehensive "how to" guide for keyboardists wanting to study funk.

Chick Corea had also enjoyed much success before turning "electric." He had been recording as a leader since the mid 1960s, and 1968's *Now He Sings, Now He Sobs* had firmly entrenched him in the jazz world as a leader that would be hard to follow. Corea also collaborated with Gary Burton (vibraphone) on the classic LP *Crystal Silence* in 1972. One year later, however, *Light as a Feather* featured Chick only on electric piano (Fender Rhodes), and seemed to be his official foray into fusion. The personnel was listed as a band with the name Return to Forever (RTF). Also, in 1973 there was yet another landmark recording from Chick Corea's new group RTF, the album *Hymn of the Seventh Galaxy*. On this LP there was a new lineup, and instead of Latin-jazz fusion, it was more aggressive, sounding like rock jazz music.

While there was a lot of music coming from America, other countries made significant contributions too, and just as in the early days of rock, English musicians were right there! Between 1971 and 1972 Emerson, Lake and Palmer released four powerful albums, turning keyboardist Keith Emerson into an icon that young players everywhere tried to emulate. If a name was used to describe *their* brand of fusion, it may be something like "classical rock." However, there was no doubt in the mind of most fans that these guys were also able to improvise. King Crimson and Brand X also eventually caught the attention of jazz and rock fans, and touring became viable for groups that previously wouldn't have had much opportunity to be heard live.

The last two decades have witnessed the proliferation of the different styles that make up fusion and their own intrinsic value on popular music as a whole. Boundaries have been blurred and we hear the effects of fusion most everywhere. Rap and hip-hop might sample the verse of a jazz composition and then add "house" drums, rock bands rap, jazz soloists improvise on rock tunes, and so on. As far as jazz-rock goes, it appears that while both formats are alive and well, so too is the blending of their respective styles.

Chapter 2

INTRODUCTION TO MODES OF THE MAJOR SCALE

This book is designed to give you an introduction to jazz-rock keyboard playing. First, understanding the seven modes of the major scale is imperative. Each of these modes is derived by starting on a different note of the major scale. Every mode is a new scale with a sound of its own, upon which accompaniments and improvised solos—or even whole compositions—may be based.

The first mode is called Ionian. Ionian is formed by starting on the first note (or first *scale degree*) of the major scale; it sounds identical to the parent major scale. Example 1 shows the C Ionian mode.

Ex. 1

C Ionian

TRACK 1

Each of the modes can be outlined in several ways. One of the ways to begin hearing the properties of the mode is to play a root-position four-note chord on the first scale degree. The sound of Ionian is the sound of a major 7th chord, shown in Example 2.

Ex. 2

TRACK 2

Cmaj7

Most of the modes have additional avenues for portraying the characteristic sound. One may find that most modes have extra color added to them, and finding a triad harmony to place over the root helps to emphasize that. With Ionian, a "V over scale degree 1" is a preferred sound. In C Ionian, it will be a G major triad over a C bass note, as in Example 3.

Ex. 3

TRACK 3

G/C

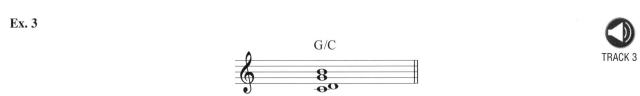

The Ionian mode, like the major scale, can be harmonized using I, IV, and V triads over each tone of the scale. Example 4 demonstrates.

Ex. 4

TRACK 4

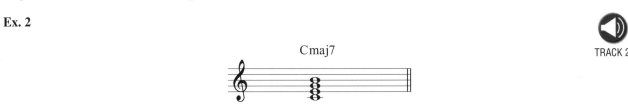

I   IV   V   I   IV   I   V   IV   V   IV   I   I

The second mode—shown in Example 5—is Dorian, which starts on the second scale degree of the major scale. In this case it will begin on D and continue up to the octave, using the notes of the C major scale.

Ex. 5

D Dorian

This mode also has a particular sound. Dorian differs from Ionian in that its third and seventh scale degrees are lowered by a half step. A four-note chord played from D (the new scale degree 1) will be the minor 7th chord in Example 6.

Ex. 6

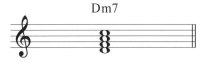

With the Ionian mode, we captured the basic sound by playing V over scale degree 1 (a G major triad with C in the bass). Now, for Dorian, let's look at Example 7. To get more familiar with the sound of this mode, try superimposing various chords over the first degree, here D. (Remember, the key signature for all of the modes discussed here is that of C major.) This example plays F major, G major, and D minor triads over the repeating bass note. The second half opens up to encompass more of the Dorian sound by adding a fourth note to each chord: in measures 3-4 we have D minor 7th, E minor 7th, and F major 7th, all over the D bass note.

Ex. 7

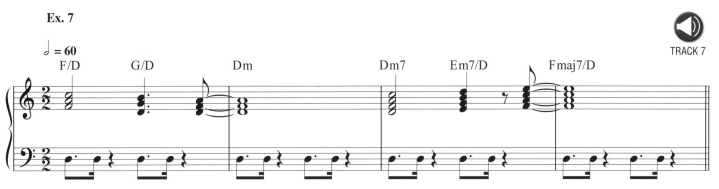

Phrygian is the third mode; so we will start on the third degree of the parent C major scale and play up for one octave, as in Example 8.

Ex. 8

E Phrygian

As with Dorian, the basic four-note chord is a minor 7th, now the Em7 of Example 9.

Ex. 9

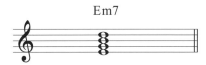

Still, Phrygian is unique. In comparison to Dorian, it has lowered second and sixth degrees; and in comparison to Ionian, it has lowered second, third, sixth, and seventh degrees. Example 10 exploits some of this uniqueness by voicing a triad built on the second degree (an F major triad) over an E bass note.

Ex. 10

TRACK 10

Example 11 adds a little bit of movement, showing how E Phrygian sounds in action. It conveys the Phrygian sound by employing simple triad voicing over a one-note bass part.

Ex. 11

TRACK 11

Moving on, the fourth mode of the major scale is called Lydian. In the key of C major, F is the fourth degree; so F to F (with a C major signature) is F Lydian, shown in Example 12. This scale differs from the Ionian in that the fourth degree is raised by a half step.

Ex. 12

F Lydian

TRACK 12

As with Ionian, the basic four-note chord outlined by Lydian is a major 7th. Example 13 shows a root-position F major 7th chord.

Ex. 13

TRACK 13

Exploring the triad harmonies can help a great deal in hearing the tonal quality of a mode. II over scale degree 1 (here a G major triad over F) is a good sound, heard in Example 14.

Ex. 14

TRACK 14

Below, in Example 15, is another pattern with some movement. Remember, Lydian sounds just like major (Ionian), except that it has a raised fourth degree.

Ex. 15

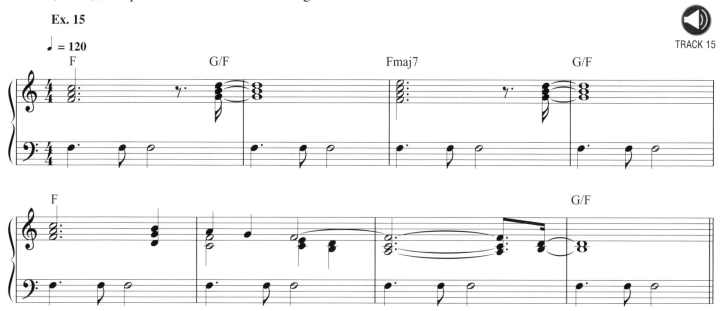

The mode in Example 16 is based upon the fifth degree of the major scale, and is known as Mixolydian: G to G, using the notes of the C major scale. Upon closer examination, you will notice that Mixolydian is a major scale with a lowered seventh degree.

Ex. 16

G Mixolydian

It is strongly recommended that you become as familiar as possible with this popular and important mode. We will visit this one again; for now, know that the root-position, four-note chord is a major triad with a minor 7th (in this case the G7 of Example 17).

Ex. 17

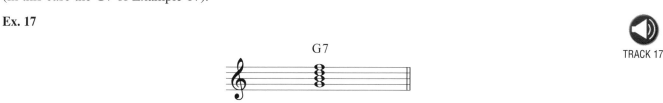

There are countless ways to approach the Mixolydian scale. A basic rock voicing is shown in Example 18, with movement that includes a suspended 4th. Notice how the alto voice plays the third, then passes through the fourth, up to the fifth of the G chord, before changing direction to return to its starting point. In the left hand, the tenor voice does something similar, moving from the fifth, through the sixth, to the seventh, then back down again.

Ex. 18

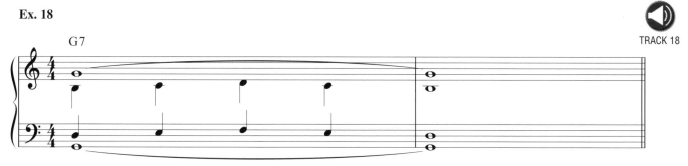

Now look at Example 19, the A Aeolian mode. The Aeolian is built from the sixth degree of the major scale. This example shows it starting on A, again using a C major key signature.

Ex. 19

 TRACK 19

A Aeolian

As in the Dorian and Phrygian modes, the primary four-note chord outlined in this mode is a minor 7th.

Ex. 20

 TRACK 20

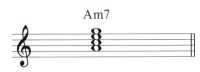

But Aeolian differs from Dorian in that it has a lowered sixth degree. Example 21 is a triad that helps us hear the properties of Aeolian: a major triad built on the sixth degree of A Aeolian, placed over scale degree 1 (here an F major triad over A in the bass).

Ex. 21

 TRACK 21

Example 22 illustrates a very typical run of notes using A Aeolian.

Ex. 22

TRACK 22

The seventh and final mode of the major scale is the Locrian mode. Using the notes of the C major scale, this mode starts on B. This mode differs from the major scale more than any other: in comparison to major it has lowered second, third, fifth, sixth, and seventh degrees. Example 23 shows B Locrian.

Ex. 23

B Locrian

The basic four-note chord that outlines this scale is a minor 7th/♭5th chord (also known as a half-diminished 7th chord). Example 24 shows this chord built on B, scale degree 1 of B Locrian.

Ex. 24

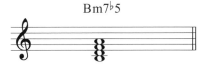

Because of the intervals contained in this type of chord, movement is usually imminent. Example 25 provides a typical progression that includes a minor 7♭5 chord. The chord progression Bm7♭5–E7♭9–Am9 is played twice.

Ex. 25

You may have realized by now that there are three basic major-sounding modes: those from the first, fourth, and fifth degrees of the major scale sound major because of the major third from the first to third note. Conversely, there are four basic minor-sounding modes: those from the second, third, sixth, and seventh degrees of the major scale are said to sound minor because of the minor third from the first to third notes. This chapter is only an introduction to these very important scales. The modes, and a few in particular, are extremely useful in playing jazz-rock keyboards. For now, see if you can become more familiar with the sound of each mode. A good exercise is to start transposing them. The next in line would be G Ionian, A Dorian, B Phrygian, etc., including every mode of the G major scale. After that, begin on the modes of D major: D Ionian, E Dorian, and so forth.

Chapter 3
CHORD VOICING

The modes discussed in the first chapter cover a lot of the scales that are used in everyday chord voicing. For now, let's take a look at two popular chord types: the major 7th and minor 7th chords. In jazz-rock, each is associated with a mode learned in Chapter 1: the major 7th chord primarily with the Ionian, and the minor 7th chord primarily with the Dorian.

Example 26 shows the four-note chord built on the first degree of the major scale (or Ionian mode), a major 7th chord in root position.

Ex. 26

TRACK 26

Learn to play every inversion of this four-note chord. In the case of a four-note chord, there is the root position, first inversion, second inversion, and third inversion, as Example 27 illustrates.

Ex. 27

TRACK 27

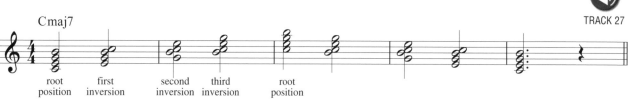

In most instances, if you are playing with a bassist, the harmonic foundation will already be covered—so using a note other than the root as the lowest pitch in the chord will sound best.

Another very popular four-note chord is the minor 7th chord. Example 28 shows a root-position minor 7th chord on D.

Ex. 28

TRACK 28

As always, learn each inversion. This is a necessity both for playing and writing music. Practice ascending, then come back down in reverse.

Ex. 29

TRACK 29

Once you feel comfortable with the basic properties, start experimenting with other scale tones added to each chord. Sometimes in jazz or jazz-rock music, chords become quite dense with these added tones, creating more harmonic power. Chord progressions come in many shapes and sizes, and we will delve more deeply into richer harmonies later. For now, be clear on the major 7th and minor 7th sounds.

When you combine elements of two or more styles, in essence you are creating a fusion. This is a simple explanation of why a very popular musical style has taken on the name "fusion." Jazz-rock combines elements of both rock and jazz; therefore, it truly is a fusion genre. At its beginning in the late 1960s, musicians who were accomplished jazz players wanted to branch out. One desirable part of rock 'n' roll was the energy. Rock bands were typically much more visual and played with a sense of urgency rarely found in jazz. One of the characteristics borrowed by jazzers was the way rock musicians organized the chord tones or voiced the chords. Instead of the clusters and spreads used in be-bop and swing, fusion started using a lot of three-note harmonies (*triads*). Often this meant placing a three-note chord over a separate bass note. Example 30 shows a G triad (G–B–D) over a C bass note. This is known as G/C (G triad over C bass). Through experimentation, I have come to the conclusion that I like this chord played with the triad portion voiced in its second inversion.

Ex. 30

TRACK 30

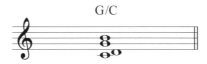

To depict the major 7th sound, try moving back and forth between two triads over a single bass note. In Example 31, an overall Cmaj7 sound is achieved by using G major and F major triads on top of the C bass. The triads are also inverted to add some variety.

Ex. 31

TRACK 31

Triadic harmonies are used widely and in varied situations in jazz-rock. Let's now take a look at them in a minor 7th chord setting. Sometimes one triad superimposed over a root isn't enough all by itself. In the case of a minor 7th chord, if you want to outline the sound with triads, you may use the major triads with roots a minor 3rd and perfect 4th above the root of the minor 7th chord. So if you see the symbol for a D minor 7th chord, you might alternate F major and G major triads over a D bass pedal. Example 32 shows this in action.

Ex. 32

TRACK 32

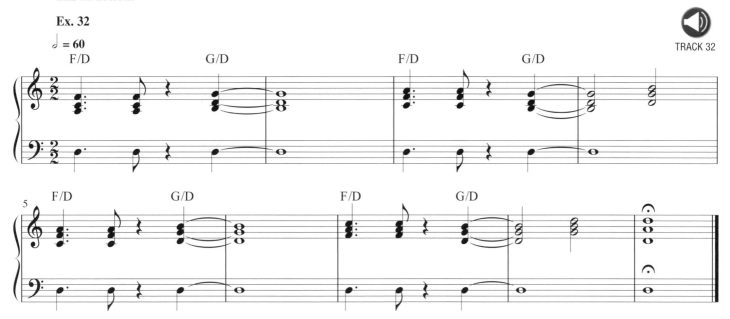

Just to give a hint of how much the sound can be changed, Example 33 plays F6 and G6 chords over a D bass.

Ex. 33

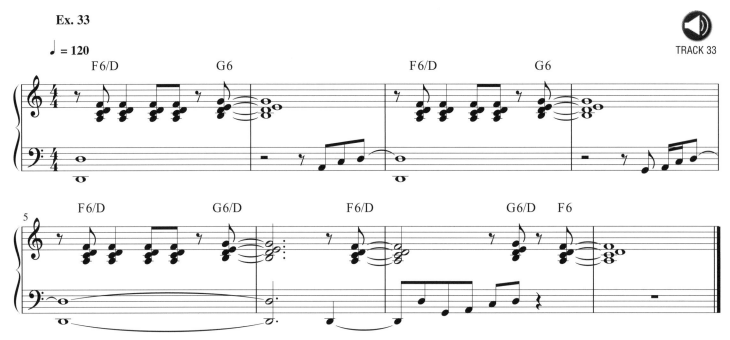

Major and minor chords can complement one another within a progression. Many jazz-rock tunes use vamps that consist of just two chords. A commonly used vamp alternates major 7th and minor 7th chords. Example 34 simply repeats Amaj7 and Bm7, back and forth. Notice how the inversion in the right hand in bar 4 adds a lift to the second half of the phrase.

Ex. 34

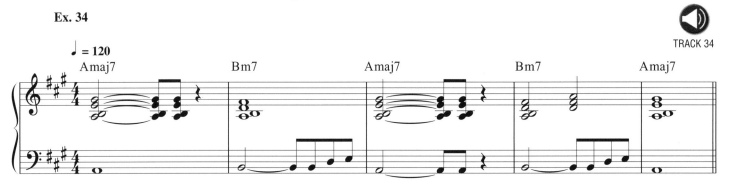

Example 35 is similar in that it is made up of a two-chord vamp: Dmaj7 and Am9. The first four bars are spelled out clearly, in a simple format. Starting at bar 5, a more rhythmic line begins out of these right-hand chords.

Ex. 35

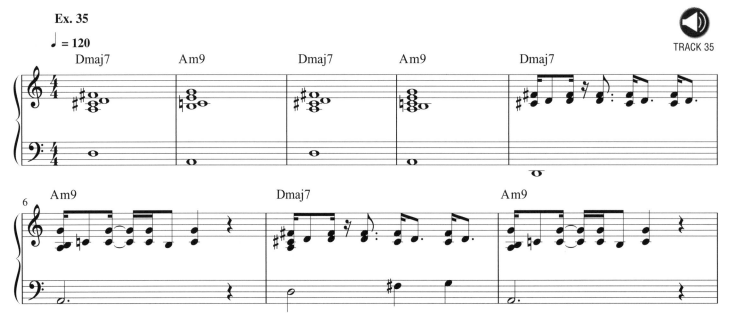

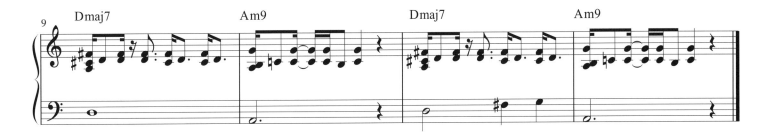

Next, listen to and compare the two chords in Example 36. What sets them apart is the order in which the chord tones appear (*voicing*), combined with the fact that the second chord uses the major 3rd and major 7th. The first one would be notated as C(add9)(no3rd), while the second one would be Cmaj9. When players use the first notation, essentially they are asking for a C triad with the 9th (or 2nd) replacing the major 3rd. The second notation tells us that the other chord tones are desirable to use as well.

Ex. 36

TRACK 36

This is just the very beginning of what are called color tones. In many types of jazz and rock, chord tones are added (as replacements or supplements) to produce more interesting sounds. We will concentrate more on this throughout the book.

Chapter 4

MIXOLYDIAN AND DORIAN IN CONTEXT

In most popular styles of music, including jazz-rock, there are chords filled with color tones (7ths, 9ths, 11ths, and 13ths) and/or harmonic alterations achieved by using clusters of notes, triadic harmonies over different bass notes, or modes. Once you see a chord or chord symbol, you need to be able to construct single-note lines for composing or improvising melodies. One of the modes we learned in Chapter 1 is the Mixolydian. This scale can also be thought of as a major scale with a flatted seventh degree, which makes it perfect for use over a dominant 7th chord. Look at the next example. Here, over an A7 harmony, I improvised a melody as an example of how lines can be constructed entirely from the scale tones, as demonstrated most obviously in bar 1. The remainder of Example 37 outlines the A Mixolydian mode. You can actually start to make music just by using scale tones and your ear!

TRACK 37

Ex. 37

Sometimes what you *don't* play helps the overall sound of a chord or scale. Pentatonic scales (five-note scales) are everywhere in jazz-rock. For now, look at the next two examples. Example 38 shows the major pentatonic scale (also called the "country-rock scale") starting on A.

TRACK 38

Ex. 38

A Major Pentatonic

Example 39 offers some riffing based solely on this scale. After a few measures I start to include the remaining notes (D and G) from the A Mixolydian scale. The major pentatonic scale by itself can be used over both major 7th and dominant 7th chords; thus, for instance, the A major pentatonic scale is appropriate to Amaj7 or A7.

Ex. 39

TRACK 39

There are several pentatonic scales that are used in jazz-rock keyboard playing. Example 40 gives the E dominant pentatonic scale, one of my favorites!

Ex. 40

TRACK 40

E Dominant Pentatonic

Because this scale has both a major 3rd and a minor 7th above scale degree 1, it clearly outlines E7. In essence, the dominant pentatonic is the Mixolydian mode without the second and sixth scale degrees. This scale has been responsible for helping to create some of the most enduring melodies in jazz-rock. In Example 41, as done previously, I will run the scale and then begin to improvise a melody using only these scale tones.

Ex. 41

TRACK 41

Now let's take a look at some common minor 7th sounds. Of course, the basic four-note chord consists of a minor 3rd, perfect 5th, and minor 7th above the root. In Example 42 it is shown with D as the root, making this a D minor 7th chord.

Ex. 42

TRACK 42

Example 43 shows two things: the D Dorian mode and the D natural minor scale.

Ex. 43

TRACK 43

D Dorian

D Natural Minor

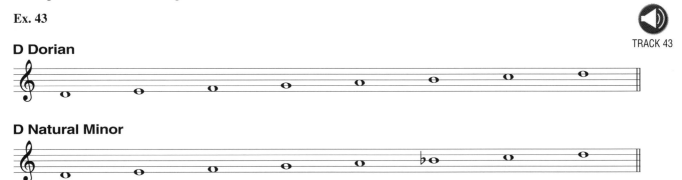

In general, jazz-rock uses the Dorian mode over a minor 7th chord. Minor 7th chords also invite the use of both the minor pentatonic and blues scales. Example 44 shows the D minor pentatonic scale, while Example 45 gives the D blues scale. The latter is simply the minor pentatonic with the added ♯4 (G♯ in the case of D minor).

Ex. 44

TRACK 44

D Minor Pentatonic

Ex. 45

D Blues

The blues progression plays an enormous role in both composition and improvisation within the jazz-rock idiom. Example 46 demonstrates how you can make your way through a simple twelve-bar blues using only these scales!

Ex. 46

TRACK 46

With regard to soloing (improvisation), there is a lot more to do and learn with the blues scale and its related scales and chord progressions. For now, however, it's time to make sure you are solid as an accompanist!

Chapter 5
ALTERNATE CHORD VOICING

Before stepping out and shining as a soloist, it is imperative that you be able to back up other play-ers. There are countless ways to approach accompaniment, or *comping*. This chapter will give you some tools for playing more interesting accompanying chords, with solid rhythm.

One of the things that I do on a regular basis is pit the left hand against the right. More intricate rhythms are created by utilizing the thumb of my left hand in opposition to the right hand, as in Example 47.

Ex. 47

TRACK 47

All good musicians mentally subdivide the beat into smaller parts so that playing can be much more precise rhythmically. So when playing a pattern that uses eighth notes, try hearing the sixteenth-note subdivisions to yourself (or if playing a shuffle or swing beat, use triplet subdivision). That is how something like Example 47 is played best!

Let's continue with the same approach. Example 48 alternates G7 and F7 chords. The harmony is relatively simple (straight dominant 7th sounds, with occasional suspended 4ths), so the rhythmic approach has been spiced up with some sixteenth-note subdivisions (and even an occasional sixteenth-note triplet). This illus-trates comping in a "pattern" format, where one creates an idea for an accompaniment, embellishes only a little, and then repeats the pattern.

Ex. 48

TRACK 48

Another way to accomplish the same result when more variety is desired is to establish a basic pattern, then break up both rhythm and harmony, as in Example 49. Note the use of triadic harmonies in the second portion of the example. This is an approach that was originally found only in rock music, but was later borrowed by jazzers for use in jazz-rock.

Ex. 49

The next two examples are similar to the preceding one. In Example 50, I played a simple rock progression of Gm9–Am9–Dm9. Note the "straight ahead" sound, with very little syncopation. In Example 51, I played the same chords, using a choppy sixteenth-note subdivision, and adding syncopation. I also used some chord inversions, climbing up in the second half of the example. Example 51 is more indicative of jazz-rock because... well, look at the name of this genre: Jazz + rock. Jazz typically uses improvisatory techniques, while rock implies a certain attitude. jazz-rock emerged as a result of combining these two styles, and examples like these will help you to retrace the footsteps of the pioneering musicians who created it!

Ex. 50

TRACK 50

Ex. 51

TRACK 51

Deciding which voicing to use when comping is something that will eventually become second nature. For starters, you should know as many types of chord structures as possible. After being able to play chords in their root positions, the next step is to learn all of the inversions. An exercise that aids in the transition from practicing to making music is shown in Example 52. In this progression (which uses only three basic chords: C7, F7, and G7), only chord tones are played in the right hand; however, they are constantly moving around to other voicings or inversions. A key to benefiting from this type of practice is to go to the nearest available voicing at each chord change—a technique used by professionals most of the time.

Ex. 52

TRACK 52

One more demonstration is necessary before moving on. We know that playing chords in different configurations or voicings adds variety and personality to the accompaniment. Also worth remembering is that if there is a bass player involved (or if the roots are being played by someone else), we needn't use every chord tone in a part. For example, in a vamp using A7 and D7#9, try leaving out the roots of each chord. Another important technique involves playing the chord tones out of order. In other words, if D7#9 is comprised of D–F#–A–C–E#, don't play it like that! Instead, arrange the tones in some other sequence. How about the famous Hendrix chord that guitar players use (F#–C–E#)? This translates wonderfully to keyboards, and we use it almost as much as they do! Now to take this concept one step further, how about a voicing like this: E#–F#–C? This introduces a *cluster* into the part, meaning that there are two (or more) notes very close together in the chord voicing (like the minor 2nd E#–F# in this case)—a type of playing found more in jazz and jazz-rock than in other popular styles. Lastly, once you have established your basic voicing, try arpeggiating the chord tones, perhaps adding some rhythmic syncopation. Remember that jazz is an improvisatory art, based around explorations. In rock, a consistent pattern may be preferable, but in jazz-rock we mix things up a bit.

Ex. 53

TRACK 53

Chapter 6
IMPROVISING OVER CHANGES: PART I

Most musicians are required to improvise, or solo, over the songs they write or play. For as long as rock music has been around, there have been solos taken regularly, especially after the vocal statement. Jazz is similar to rock, in that solos are expected here also. As a matter of fact, jazz players like to improvise a lot, taking long solos, "stretching out" over changes. Any way you slice it, people expect a good player to be skilled at taking leads as well as accompanying, and in this chapter we will begin to examine what is involved in creating a good improvised lead, or solo.

A couple of elements come to mind right away: in a solo you want to make a strong statement melodically and rhythmically, with good voice leading. Sometimes it is advantageous to imagine and refer to the original written melody while soloing. Other times a radical departure seems good right away. I like to take a scalar approach, usually mixing several elements of the song at once. For starters, let's say you have a Gmaj7 chord in front of you. We can run parts of the G major (or G Ionian) scale in sections, as in Example 54.

Ex. 54

TRACK 54

Or we might use more of a chordal approach, getting ideas that stem from the four chord tones, as in Example 55.

Ex. 55

TRACK 55

Playing stylistically is paramount in creating a strong solo statement that is consistent with the piece being performed. Playing something jazzy over a rock groove may sound corny, while "rocking out" over jazz changes may likewise sound inappropriate. Look at and listen to Example 56. This is a simple melodic statement over an A7 chord, based almost entirely on the notes of the A Mixolydian mode (with a few hints of the A blues scale toward the end).

Ex. 56

TRACK 56

In particular, notice how this same passage changes drastically depending on the approach. Example 57 treats it like a rock 'n' roll melody, with straight-eighth subdivision.

Ex. 57

Next, listen to Example 58: the same notes, but sounding a lot different because of the "feel," right?

Ex. 58

For practice, try to improvise lines using the same chord changes but with different types of grooves or "feels" underneath.

Voice leading is a very important factor in creating a melodic solo. The point is to create movement not only in the accompanying chords, but also with the lead, or single-note melodic part. Using the term "lead" to refer to an improvised solo tends to suggest that the melodic part is helping to lead the listener from one chord to the next.

A good practice technique is to invent a vamp of two (or eventually more) chords; then, through the use of *common tones* (notes shared by the two chords), half steps, and whole steps, construct melodic lines that make the most sense. Example 59 vamps on Gm7 and C7, four beats each. In the first two bars, the groove is set up, which you should imagine from then on. The third and fourth bars are simple voicings of the two chords. There follows an improvised melody, beginning in measure 5.

Ex. 59

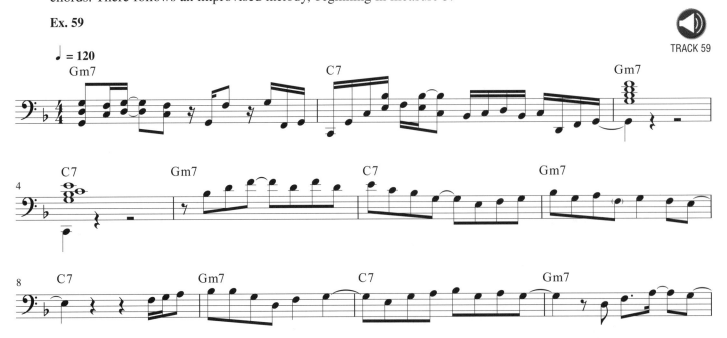

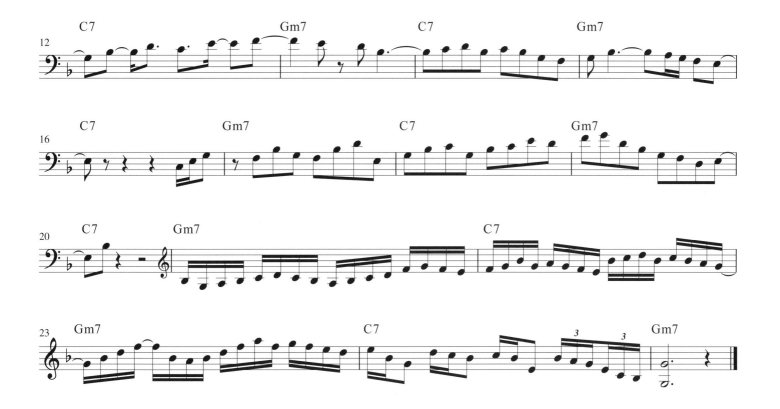

Throughout this exercise, the focus was on common tones (G and B♭ being the tones that Gm7 and C7 have in common), minor and major 3rds, and arpeggios with chord inversions. The next chapter will address "change running," a concept also used in practicing.

Although this chapter provides only an introduction to improvising, let's create a scenario that allows us to jump right in. When studying improv, the sequence may go something like this: Learn which scales fit the chords being used in the music. Next, learn the melody of the piece. Then start fusing the melody with your knowledge of scales to create your improvisation. Remember, the style you are playing is a very important factor in the outcome of a successful solo.

Now let's take a look at Example 60. Listen to it, then learn to play both the accompanying chords and the melody.

Ex. 60

TRACK 60

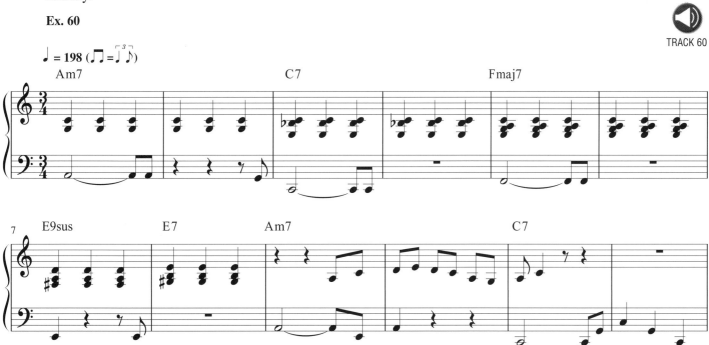

The first demonstration with this piece will embellish the melody. Listen to Example 61. This version sticks fairly close to the original melody. Keeping this melody as the main underlying force, it is decorated a bit, using scalar knowledge and rhythm to make more out of it. Note that although notes are added in this melodic-embellishment approach, it isn't always necessary. In fact, playing *less* is often more desirable!

Ex. 61

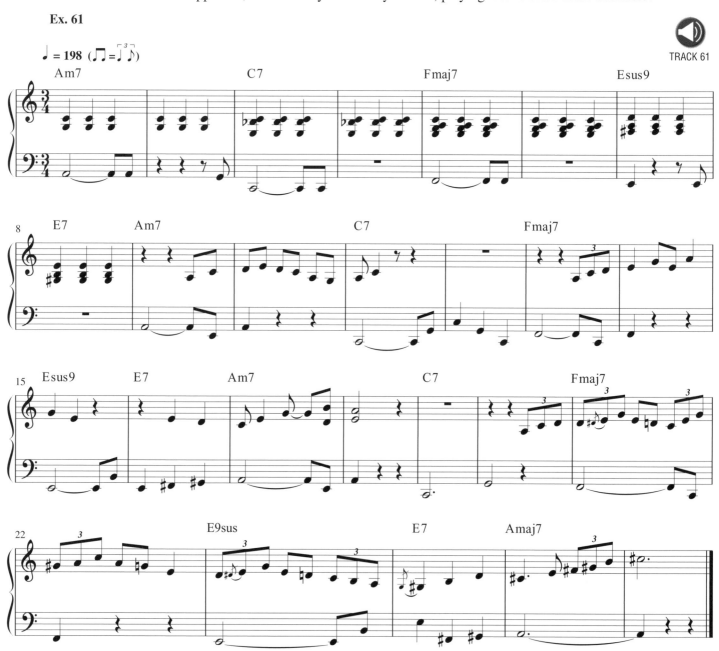

A thorough approach will also include playing scales that fit the chords. Example 62 demonstrates using simple eighth-note patterns, with both ascending and descending scales. One of the benefits of this will be the ability to lead seamlessly from one chord to the next, which will foster the improvising of longer lines over changes. This is the beginning of "change running."

There is usually more than one way to perceive the scales that are used over chord changes. In this piece, for example, the chords are Am7, C7, Fmaj7, and Esus9–E7. This time through, I thought modally, using A Dorian, C Mixolydian, F Ionian, and E Mixolydian.

Ex. 62

TRACK 62

Chapter 7

IMPROVING OVER CHANGES: PART II

Now that you have had an introduction to improvising over chord changes, let's continue along the same path in this chapter. Remember, in order to create an interesting lead, you really should know the melody, have command over which scales fit each chord, and understand the style of music being played.

Example 63 serves as the template for the next couple of exercises. This is a background part made up of four bars of E7 alternating with four bars of G7. First, let's concentrate on the rhythmic element. In order to play this accurately, you need to be able to subdivide the beat in your head down to the sixteenth note. One of the main ingredients of a great sound is the feel or groove that you lay down. This part is a good example of the syncopated jazz-rock style. Since syncopation plays such a huge role in jazz-rock, it is advisable to practice your timing continually. Make sure that you can play Example 63 with rock-solid rhythm before moving ahead.

Ex. 63

TRACK 63

Now imagine that this part is being played by a bassist, or a guitarist and bassist together. That leaves us free to improvise. We already know that two of the scales we will be able to use are E Mixolydian and G Mixolydian. You know that working out on eighth notes will have a positive affect on your ability to improvise, but how about some rhythm to spice it up a bit? Example 64 uses mostly upbeats as a method of cementing the rhythmic structure of the phrase. Notice that for phrasing purposes, a few downbeats were played to help lend some continuity to the lines.

Ex. 64

Let's continue to think about rhythm with regard to practicing single-note lines. The next example requires a bit more control. In this exercise, eighth-note triplets are played against the sixteenth-note subdivision of the bass part, continuing for several beats. The phrase ends with two beats of sixteenth notes to solidify control by returning to the same subdivision as the accompanying part. In bar 3, things get up a little more, playing an eighth and two sixteenths on each beat. The remainder of Example 65 is again eighth-note triplets mixed in with sixteenth-note scalar passages. This is an instance where there is an underlying time feel, yet on top of it the rhythm is going in and out of other superimposed time feels.

Ex. 65

There is another practice technique that can be rewarding when it comes to your time feel later on. One thing that separates proficient musicians from the rest is their control over the timing of licks and lines. Playing triplets over a straight-eighth accompaniment is an important start. But what about more advanced patterns? What about groups of, say, five notes at a time (quintuplets)? In 4/4 time, the playing of twenty quintuplet sixteenth notes in a bar, in four groups of five notes each, would do the trick. On top of that (as though it isn't difficult enough to execute evenly), how about accenting each group on a different note? In other words, in the first quintuplet, play the first note strongly. In the second group of five notes, accent the second note, and so on down the line. In 4/4 time, you will not be able to complete the pattern in a single measure, but will actually start over on beat 2 of the second bar! This type of exercise is not for beginners, but rather for keyboardists really looking to stretch their rhythmic technique. Although not for your "every-day" type of improvisation, Example 66 has been included as a reminder that we never really reach our full potential as long as we remain hungry for more knowledge and facility!

Ex. 66

TRACK 66

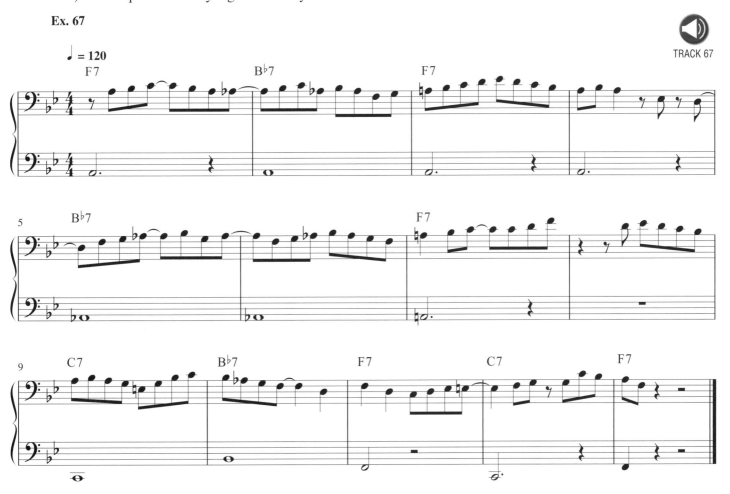

Rhythm aside, the ability to create pleasing melodic content on the spot is vital. We have looked at running scales, which is extremely important in creating long lines. Voice leading the tones of these scales is also a big deal. Jazz-rock, like other popular music styles, utilizes the blues progression (involving the harmonies I, IV, and V), or at least parts of it, in much of the music. I have spent a lot of time practicing voice leading on blues myself, and have learned a lot from it. Look at Example 67, realizing the importance of the chords' thirds and sevenths, and how they interact within the framework of good voice leading. Notice that this simple improvisation relies entirely on scale tones (the Mixolydian mode corresponding to each chord root) set in a predominantly eighth-note rhythm.

Ex. 67

TRACK 67

Okay, we know that a blues melody can be constructed using only the minor pentatonic scale, blues scale, and Mixolydian mode. But how about some extra ornamental tones? Actually, every one of the twelve tones can be used in a blues lick. In addition to the seven tones of the Mixolydian mode, there are five possible auxiliary tones. Let's go through them all, starting with the ♭9 (or ♭2). Example 68 shows a G7 chord with the non-scale tone A♭ (spelled as G♯).

If we are using G Mixolydian over G7, then the next non-scale tone is the ♯9 (or ♭3), A♯ in this case. Example 69 demonstrates what this will sound like over G7.

Ex. 69

TRACK 69

A popular half-step passing tone in this type of chord is the ♯4 (or ♯11, or ♭5). In the case of G7, it is a C♯ (or D♭). Listen now to Example 70.

Ex. 70

TRACK 70

Next in line for half-step passing tones would be the ♯5 (or ♭13), which in the context of G7 is D♯ (or E♭). This is heard in Example 71.

Ex. 71

TRACK 71

And finally, we come to the major 7th above the chord root (F♯ in the case of G7), employed in Example 72.

Ex. 72

TRACK 72

Remember that all of these half-step ornaments are used to add color to a line. They are generally not used on downbeats or in other strong rhythmic positions, though occasionally they may occur on the beat so as to delay the arrival of the main note.

Now, on to Example 73. Here we see many of the topics we have touched on already in this chapter. The chords alternate between G7 and F7. In only eight bars, we find a variety of rhythmic lines, scalar licks, and even some ornamental tones thrown in.

Ex. 73

We have spent quite a bit of the book thus far on the dominant 7th and minor 7th sounds. But jazz-rock explores new and different harmonic territory as well, so it's time to press on.

One aspect of jazz music that is used commonly in jazz-rock is the denser harmonic sound. While rock tends to use more basic chord structures, jazz-rock takes more liberties, perhaps because keyboards are often found in the instrumentation. Half steps are usually a bit cumbersome to execute harmonically on guitar, but they lie quite comfortably on a keyboard. Look at Example 74. In another style of music, this progression might read: B♭7–Am7–Gm7–C7–Fmaj7. However, you will find that adding a few clusters (half-step groupings) changes the whole sound. With just a few alterations, the harmonies have become more dense, yet they still fall rather easily under the hands of a keyboardist! The example plays B♭13–Am9–Gm9–C13♭9–C(add♭13)(add♭9)–Fmaj7♯9(♯11)–Fmaj9.

Ex. 74

Personally, I like to use triadic harmonies when appropriate. Check out a similar chord structure in Example 75, only this time, think triads over bass notes. Basically, the same denser sounding harmony can be achieved by thinking like this: C/B♭ bass, C/A bass, B♭/G bass, A/C bass, E/F bass, C/F bass. The point here is that depending on the situation you are playing in, there are numerous ways to approach a part, while still keeping the intended sound.

Ex. 75

As 7th chords are a staple of any fusion player and composer, we will outline some more examples of this nature. This time, however, let's explore a little deeper what truly makes up a jazz-rock progression, as well as some improvisational approaches. Example 76 will be our template. This short piece simply vamps between C7 and F7.

Ex. 76 – Rhodes

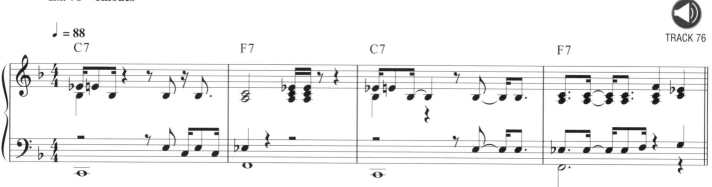

TRACK 76

This works as is, but let's go a bit further into it. Example 76 clearly outlines the dominant 7th harmonies. But in order to cross over into jazz-rock, this sound needs a little "boost" provided by some additional chord tones. Example 77 is similar, but you will see and hear how it has been changed with a little imagination. As mentioned earlier, since this feels pretty comfortable on a keyboard, adding extra or alternate chord tones can come rather easily. In this last exercise, color tones have been added to the previous dominant 7th chords. In bar 1 there is a 13 and a $\sharp$9; in the next bar, another 13 and a 9. Then on beats 3–4, passing chords B$\flat$7 and B7 have been added. The second time through the vamp, a suspended 4th, then a 13, $\flat$13, and $\flat$9 are used before going to our F7 chord again.

Ex. 77 – Rhodes

TRACK 77

Investigating new chords and melodies that fit the jazz-rock profile is best done in longer forms, such as complete songs. Let's move to Chapter 7 and put some of this to use!

Chapter 8
PUTTING IT ALL TOGETHER

This chapter is dedicated to putting into action what has been covered previously. Let's take a look at some examples in song form. Example 78 provides opportunities to use the Dorian, Mixolydian, and blues scales. Jazz-rock songs often are vehicles for jamming, as this one is. In fact, some of the most memorable music of this genre was actually created to feature the playing as much as the writing.

After a vamp and quick melody statement, the song modulates up a whole step to sit for a while on Am7. This is typical of this kind of music, as is the fact that the Am7 is outlined with a unison lick, adding strength. Often jazz-rock's power stems from just this kind of approach: a modulation, followed by a strong unison line. For a turnaround back to Gm7, I progress up to the V chord of G (here D7#9), and then to F7, which moves to another unison statement (this one based on Gm7) from a step below.

Ex. 78

TRACK 78

After reviewing Example 78, move on to the next tune. Example 79 shows a mostly right-hand melodic lead (improv), based on the melody. In order to fit in with the style and overall feel and sound of this piece, the line sticks to a G blues scale, with a touch of G Dorian for the first twelve bars. Then the song moves up in bar 13 to A minor pentatonic, A blues, and A Dorian. Note: for added "personality," try superimposing a D dominant pentatonic scale over the Am7 in bars 13–16. This adds a different flair to the minor 7th sound, actually creating a minor (add13)(add11) harmony.

Ex. 79

TRACK 79

Now it's your turn! After examining my note choices in Example 79, start practicing over these changes yourself. Example 80 shows the basic changes one time through. However, the audio example keeps on going, allowing you to try different scales, licks, etc., over the chords.

Ex. 80 – Rhodes

TRACK 80

Example 81 is an original song that has appeared on two different recordings, with two different approaches. "Crystal" was first recorded in a mellow jazzy setting, and then later done with some distorted guitar, turning it into a jazz-rock piece.

Let's take a look at the intro. Here a C pedal supports movement on top. The first chord is Cm9, followed by D♭maj7 (over the C bass). Next is a C7sus4(add13), and the last chord is a quasi-G7♯9, again over a C bass. On the final bar of the intro (bar 8), the bass moves to G to create a definitive G7, which leads nicely into the verse.

The main melody, beginning in bar 9, moves over a descending bass line, and the harmonies above connect via some common tones. The next section (measures 17–24) is a study in triadic harmony. By having the bass part play an ascending line, I was able to repeat similar triads while still changing the sound harmonically. Track 81 plays the form twice, as noted below, then continues on, ad libitum.

Crystal
Version 1

TRACK 81

Ex. 81

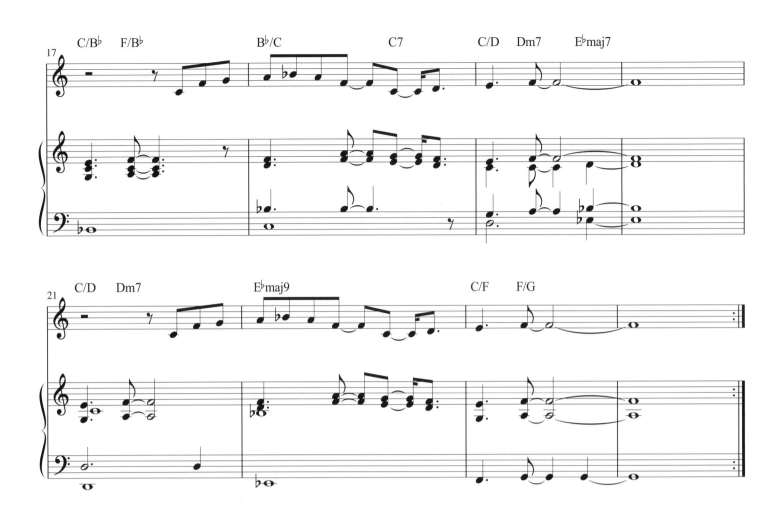

On the second recording of "Crystal" we used the first solo section for a keyboard solo, and the vamp-out at the end for wailing guitar. The first solo section shares some of the verse's harmonies, but also adds a bit of mixed meter as well. This is Example 82. The second improv section you can work on is the ending vamp, shown in Example 83. On both examples, the audio continues to vamp to give you some time to practice.

Crystal
Version 2

Ex. 82 – Rhodes

TRACK 82

Ex. 83 – Rhodes

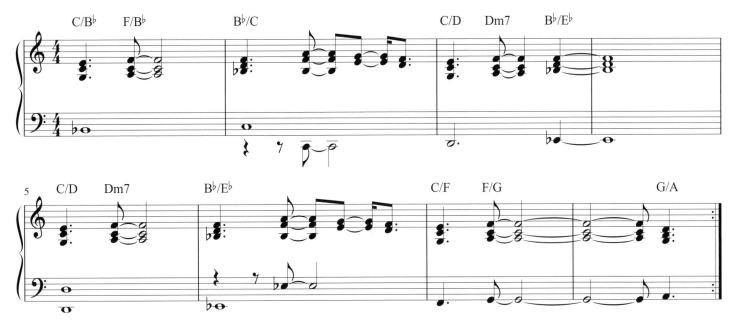

Chapter 9
DIFFERENT APPROACHES TO DIFFERENT KEYBOARDS

When I used to play saxophone, I noticed that although all of the different horns (alto, tenor, etc.) shared a similar sound, the way players approached each one was a lot different. The sound of a baritone sax lends itself to more root-oriented parts, while the higher-pitched instruments are better at melodies. Nothing is absolute, but it does seem to work like this in general.

Luckily, I come from a generation of keyboard players that began lessons on piano. That was mainly by default, as the other keyboards that have now become so popular weren't really around back then! I feel good about this background because I appreciate the natural sound and feel of an acoustic instrument, yet I can also enjoy today's technology.

It was predominantly in the 1970s that the electric piano (mostly the Rhodes and Wurlitzer) became entrenched in the modern sound. These two keyboards can be used for almost any part. First, let's look at the issue of chord voicings. Whereas single- and double-note parts are best suited to a clavinet or punchy synth sound, the electric pianos can really dominate a piece with larger chord groups (more notes in a chord). Notice in Example 84 that the left hand often doubles the bass notes (if you do this, be sure that the bass is playing a written part and not improvising, or it won't work).

Ex. 84

TRACK 84

44

Another favorite tactic in playing a jazz-rock electric piano part is to accent snare drum hits. In Example 85 the last two hits in bar 4 coincide with what the drummer is playing. With a good electric piano sound, it is also often desirable and appropriate to play high bell-like sounds using some notes of the chord.

Ex. 85 – Rhodes

TRACK 85

An instrument that must be thought of differently than the piano or electric piano is the clavinet. A combination of brash timbre and harsh attack make this instrument perfect for accenting rhythm parts. Typically the clavinet is not used in ballads or lush, slow-moving pieces (unless an underlying rhythmic subdivision of the beat is desired). Our first clavinet demonstration, Example 86, enlivens an E7 harmony. This is a popular type of part for me over any dominant 7th, and the way to play it is by pitting the thumb of the left hand against fingers 1–4 of the right hand. In this case, the upper E is repeated by the fourth finger of the right hand, while fingers 3, 2, and 1 play the D, C♯, and B. It is important to leave space in a clavinet part, so the music can breathe.

Ex. 86 – Clavinet

TRACK 86

Although the clavinet is not often thought of as a solo instrument, it really does sound good doing a bit of everything, including improv. In Example 87, the Wurlitzer is doing the main comping part. Listen, however, as the clavinet accentuates the bass by playing roots, and answers the other keyboard playing the top part. Obviously, most live situations will feature a guitarist before a second keyboardist, so you might imagine the Wurlitzer part played on guitar.

Ex. 87

TRACK 87

Organ is another important instrument in the arsenal of the complete jazz-rock keyboardist. While this instrument became popular in other musical arenas first, all kinds of musicians use it nowadays. Everything from jazz to rock, Latin to country—you name it, and this instrument's presence is felt. Organ—especially the real thing, Hammond organ—was one of my first loves, after acoustic piano.

A great-sounding organ is inspiring to play, and can be used effectively not only for long, sustained parts, but for percussive, choppy, rhythmic ones, too. Adding more attack to your organ sound will help with the latter. Of course, on a real organ there is the percussion selection, and that—like all of the knobs, switches, and drawbars—will affect your overall organ sound. It is recommended you engage in lots of experimentation in order to familiarize yourself with all of these functions; that is really the best way to get command of the many sound options. Example 88 shows how the right and left hands can create a wonderful combined sound that adds lots of rhythm to a track. Note: Set the left hand (lower manual) to a lighter sound; this will help strengthen the right hand.

Ex. 88 – Organ

TRACK 88

One of the big adjustments that a piano player has to make in order to sound good on organ concerns the sustain. Real organs don't have a sustain pedal, so the sustain comes only from the fingers. By increasing the amount of sustain I create with my fingers on the organ, I have actually helped my piano chops as well. This is important, as you want your delivery to be as smooth as possible.

Example 89 is a typical triadic organ part. To keep it smooth, try replacing fingers that trigger a chord with new ones that sustain. This will enable you to strike the next chord in a legato fashion. For example, in the third bar, there are three inversions of an F major triad in the right hand. If the second chord is played with fingers 2, 3, and 5, while holding the chord replace 2 with 1, 3 with 2, and 5 with 3. This will allow you to finger the last F chord with 2, 3, and 5 again. In the left hand, try playing the second low B♭ with your little finger, and then while holding it, substitute your third finger. When the movement down to A occurs, slide down with the same third finger. You can then play G with your fourth finger, and the low E♭ with your little finger. If all of this is done correctly, it will sound as though you have a sustain pedal!

Ex. 89 – Organ

Organ is a great instrument for accompaniments and solos. Sometimes it can be used for both, as is evident in Example 90. Listen as the bass line is doubled and harmonized, and note the right hand's improvised melodic fills.

Ex. 90 – Organ

The great thing about soloing on organ is that you can accompany yourself with left-hand chords in a pleasing register, so as to complement the solo part. Example 91 actually shows the instrument being used as a one-man band. With a good setup, you can accompany with both harmony (left-hand chords) and bass (pedals). Although this is not too easily accomplished with older technology, today's devices make it possible to simulate all of the components of a real organ.

Ex. 91

TRACK 91

Clavinet and organ are great for band orchestration. Whether or not you are privileged enough to have the real instruments at hand, both lead and backing parts can be made with a myriad of sounds. On a synthesizer you can approximate some other really good sounds, like strings and horns. Take the time to listen to how your favorite players approach these sounds. Whether it is an accentuating punch or a smooth, spacey mix, the possibilities for synth sounds seem to be limitless; if you use your ears, you will be able to tap into as many as you need.

One of the primary areas that the consummate jazz-rock keyboardist will want to master is the lead synth. It is important to learn about the different sounds popular in this idiom, and to be able to double melodies and solo using this approach. Example 92 demonstrates one of the most popular approaches to playing lead synthesizer, as it infuses the melodic lines with pitch bends, produced by a modulation wheel (older synthesizers used levers, ribbons, and joysticks). A solo like this one usually has the keyboardist setting the pitch bend to "2" (meaning *two semitones*).

Ex. 92 – Synth Lead

Lead synthesizers like the classic Moog have a very particular sound, both cutting and pleasing (depending on how it is programmed and processed), which is great for doubling a melody or doing fills around it. Hear how, in Example 93, the mellow-sounding patch (playing mostly single-note parts) strengthens the melody and complements it with fills.

The last lead-synth patch demo, Example 94, shows how a jazz-rock keyboardist can shine as simultaneous accompanist and soloist. With the left hand on a lower-manual keyboard (bottom keyboard on a two-tier stand) playing chords, and the right hand doing the melodic improv, you can do interesting things like "sidestepping" the changes, and generally lay down a strong foundation for each solo lick or phrase you play.

Ex. 94